buddy

BASED ON THE TRUE STORY
OF GERTRUDE LINTZ

WILLIAM JOYCE

A LAURA GERINGER BOOK
AN IMPRINT OF HARPER COLLINS PUBLISHERS

Special thanks to Stephanie Allain and Brian Henson and all the
gang at the Henson Company; Fred Fuchs, Francis Coppola, and
Elisabeth Seldes; Steve Nicolaides; and lastly, Caroline Thompson

Library of Congress Cataloging-in-Publication Data
Joyce, William.
Buddy / by William Joyce
p.   cm.
"Based on the true story of Gertrude Lintz."
"A Laura Geringer book."
Summary: Gertrude Lintz, a New York socialite who believes that animals
should not be caged, raises a gorilla named Buddy and reluctantly realizes that he
is not suited for city life.
ISBN 0-06-027660-6
1. Lintz, Gertrude—Juvenile fiction. [1. Lintz, Gertrude—Fiction.
2. Gorilla—Fiction. 3. Animals—Treatment—Fiction.] I. Title.
PZ7.J857Bu 1997   97-2801
[Fic]—dc21   CIP
                                                                                              AC

Designed by Christine Kettner
1 2 3 4 5 6 7 8 9 10
❖
First Edition

To John LaViolette and Michael Siegel,
amiable compadres in the
perfidious land to the West.

CHAPTER I

a long time ago, in the 1930's, you might have seen many amazing things, for it was an amazing time.

There were people who would sit at the tops of flagpoles for weeks at a time—some would sing songs, some would dance, others would balance on their heads for as long as they could, just so they would be noticed.

There were people who were so poor they had no money for food, so they would dance in contests. They would do funny dances called the "Lindy Hop" or the "Jitterbug" for days and days without stopping. The point of the contest wasn't to see who could dance the best but who could dance the longest, and whoever won would get money for food. There was even a couple who danced all the way across the country from New York to Los Angeles!

There were men and women who walked on the wings of flying airplanes and played tennis. There were people who shot themselves out of cannons. And a famous writer and his wife used to play in a fountain wearing only their pajamas.

The sky was filled with airships called dirigibles, great balloons with propellers, the largest machines ever to fly.

There were people who lost everything they had, so they roamed the open road, desperate for a friend, a meal, or a place to call home.

There were movies like *King Kong* and *The Wizard of Oz*, and the biggest film star in the world was a little girl named Shirley Temple.

It was a time when men wore hats and women gloves, when gangsters had Tommy guns, and rich ladies drank champagne from their slippers. And the music on the radio was as sweet and happy as any ever heard.

It was a glorious, sad, and amazing time.

And if you happened to be walking down the street in New York City in the 1930's, you might have seen one of the most amazing things of all—a beautiful woman with a very well-dressed, full-grown gorilla sporting a red carnation in the lapel of his jacket. The lady's name? Gertie Lintz. And the gorilla's name was Buddy.

But how does a gorilla come all the way from Africa to be on the streets of New York wearing a suit and a tie and a red flower in his lapel? Well, here's the story.

buddy was the youngest gorilla in the jungle. His father was a leader. His mother was powerful and kind. They roamed the jungle freely and unafraid. As they foraged for food, Buddy's mother would hold him close and feed him while his father stood guard. There were many dangers in the jungle, and Buddy was just beginning to learn. If he fell into a lake or pond he'd drown, since gorillas cannot swim. If he wandered too far he'd be easy prey for leopards or panthers—or men. Buddy had not yet seen a man. He knew nothing of their world. He knew only the verdant shade and lazy comforts of his home and the safety of his parents' arms.

But one night there were torches and gunfire in the dark. Buddy and his parents huddled in the shadows. The men came closer and closer. His father charged, but shots rang out, and he fell to the ground. His mother let out a furious scream. Buddy clutched her tightly around the neck as she hurtled through the line of men, tossing them aside like rag dolls. As she ran across a shallow stream, shots rang out again. She crashed to the watery ground. Pinned beneath her, Buddy could not move. He could barely breathe as water from the stream washed over him. He could see the men as they came closer. Then everything went black, and Buddy would not wake up again for a long, long time.

Mrs. Gertrude Lintz was an amazing woman.

Born in England, she sailed to America on an ocean liner when she was only a little girl.

Young Gertie had ten brothers and sisters. On their journey they had confused America with Africa when looking at the maps in the captain's atlas. They thought America would be filled with lions and elephants and gorillas. They were disappointed when they found only cows and horses and chickens in the barn on their new farm.

Gertie's father had been a great opera singer, but his voice had grown weak, and he could no longer sing a whole opera, only an aria or two. Her mother was a fine pianist, but the family had fallen on hard times. When they inherited a farm in America it was decided that the family would try life in a whole new country.

Gertie sometimes missed her home in England, but she grew to love her life on the farm. She spent all her spare time with the animals. Sometimes in the late afternoon when all the chores were done, her father would sing a bit of opera while her mother played the piano. Gertie would sit on the lawn with her animals and listen to the music. None of her animals were

caged. She couldn't bear to lock them up. So they played around her as the music drifted through the rarefied air of those grand and gentle days.

But when Gertie was twelve her mother died of typhoid fever. Her father fell into despair and could no longer care for the children. Gertie and her ten brothers and sisters were split up and sent away to different farms.

The farmers in her new home were stern and cheerless. There was no music or pets. Gertie felt trapped.

So one day Gertie ran away to the forest.

Finding food and shelter as best she could, she lived like a wild thing for as long as she could. And in that time she came to understand animals as few people ever do.

She decided that when she grew up she would never again live in a house without animals. And true to her word, when Gertie grew up, her house was full of animals.

She had four chimpanzees: two girls and two boys. The boys were named Joe Mendi and Captain Jiggs. The girls were named Skippy and Maggie Klein. She had a leopard named Boo

Joe Mendi

and a Komodo dragon named Lawrence who usually hid under the couch in the living room. There were a number of magnificent dogs, including her favorite, a little dachshund named Lancelot, who wore glasses.

Lancelot

There were horses, a whole pavilion of birds, including a talking parrot named Charlie, hundreds of tropical fish, and countless exotic butterflies that flickered around the vast estate. But there was one animal Gertie did not have that she had always wanted: a gorilla.

Dick and Beulah

a baby gorilla!" Gertie whispered excitedly as she rushed to her car.

"Where are you going?" asked her husband, Dr. Bill Lintz, who was setting up the croquet set on the lawn.

"To the Philadelphia Zoo to get a gorilla!" she shouted as she drove away.

"Did she say to 'get a gorilla' or 'get some vanilla'?" Bill asked Dick, the animal trainer.

"I think it was gorilla," he replied.

"I *know* she said gorilla!" grumbled Beulah, the house-keeper.

"Gorilla! Gorilla! Gorilla!" chimed in Charlie, the parrot.

"Oh, well then," muttered Bill as he went back to his wickets, "you should set another place at the table, Beulah. I guess a gorilla will be coming to dinner."

But by the time Gertie got home that evening, dinner was finished and everyone had gone to bed.

Carefully she carried Buddy into the downstairs den. He was wrapped in a towel and was sleeping in small open crate. His breathing was hoarse and ragged.

She sat by the fireplace and tried to feed Buddy with a baby's bottle. "Please take it, Buddy," she said gently. "You've got to eat."

She began to hum a song her mother used to play on the piano. Her voice was soft and lovely and carried through the house like a sigh. Then one by one the chimps wandered in.

They were dressed in their pajamas. Joe Mendi held his red blanket close.

Soon Lancelot the dog walked in with Charlie the parrot on his back. Then came Dr. Lintz and Dick the trainer and Beulah. They gathered around Gertie and the tiny gorilla.

Joe handed him his red blanket. The other chimps tucked

it around him and stroked his head. Skippy held his hand.

Buddy looked up at this strange group. He clutched the red blanket with one hand and began to take milk from the bottle.

"Good boy," Gertie whispered. "Welcome to your new home, Buddy." And she kissed him on the forehead.

And for the first time since he'd left the jungle, Buddy did not feel sad or lonely or afraid. He felt almost at home.

CHAPTER 4

Weeks passed, and every day Buddy became stronger and stronger. But the task of caring for him had left Gertie very tired. One day Buddy hugged her tightly around the neck and would not let go. No matter what anyone tried, no one could make him let go. So Gertie ate breakfast with Buddy around her neck. When she went shopping, Buddy went along and wouldn't let go. Not even for animal crackers. Gertie ate lunch with Buddy around her neck. Dinner was the same. When she slept that night he never let go, even in his sleep.

The next morning Gertie tried to take a bath, and Buddy finally let go. As she turned on the water, he screamed and struggled to get away. Gertie tried to calm him, but he cried so long and loud that everyone in the house came to see what was wrong. Luckily Joe Mendi had brought Buddy's red blanket, and as soon as Gertie wrapped him in it he quieted.

"Poor thing," she said. "He's afraid of the water."

"Well, at least you can get some rest," said Bill.

"For now," said Beulah.

"Red blanket! Red blanket!" trilled Charlie.

"Red blanket, indeed!" said Gertie.

And from then on, whenever she needed help with Buddy, she'd bring out his red blanket and he'd calm down.

"You're such a mystery," Gertie said to Buddy as she rocked him to sleep that night. "My lovely little mystery."

buddy ate so much that Gertie and Bill bought him his own refrigerator. He loved bananas, grapes, and strawberry pie. For breakfast he could eat a whole box of cereal, dough-nuts by the dozen, entire loaves of bread, and gallons of apple juice and still be hungry.

The Lintzes were used to serving vast amounts of all kinds of foods to their ani-mals. Insects, fungus, or Italian food—the animals ate it all.

"If it crawls, grows, flies, or wig-gles, I've cooked it or served it," grumbled Beulah. But Buddy was her favorite. "At least he doesn't eat anything weird," she said.

Buddy became everyone's favor-ite. He was happy, curious, and lively. "He's like the sweetest little kid you've ever seen," said Bill one day. But Buddy did not stay little for long. In a few months he'd outgrown the chimps. In a year he was the size of a ten-year-old boy. By the time he was three he was bigger than a man.

"Well, at least he can wear my hand-me-downs," said Dr. Lintz, whose waistline spoke of one who found great joy and contentment at the dinner table.

But Buddy soon outgrew even the doctor's suits! Now Gertie would have to have his clothes made to order.

Dick drove them all into New York City one sunny October day. They went straight to Bergdorf Goodman's, the finest store in town.

Otto, the doorman at Bergdorf's, was used to seeing Mrs. Lintz with her chimps, but his jaw dropped when he saw Buddy.

"What ya been feeding this one, Mrs. Lintz, that he would get so big?" he asked.

"He's not a chimp, Otto," she replied calmly. "He's a gorilla. His name is Buddy."

"With a Buddy like that I guess you don't have any enemies!" Otto laughed as he held open the door.

People in every department of the store were a little unnerved by the sight of a full-grown gorilla picking out hats and being fitted for Sunday suits and play clothes. Gertie herself was nervous about Buddy. She kept his red blanket at the ready in case he got excited.

"Shouldn't he be on a leash or something?" quavered the salesman at the tie counter.

"Oh, don't be silly," replied Gertie. "Just give me all your red neckties, and he'll be fine." Buddy beat his chest joyfully.

The salesman quickly obliged, and Gertie bought every red tie in the store. She even bought Buddy a red carnation for the lapel of his new overcoat.

As they were leaving, Buddy saw a mannequin wearing a beautiful red coat and hat in the ladies' department. He picked up the mannequin and began to carry it out.

"Well, I guess I've been needing a new outfit," said Gertie. "How about I wear it instead of the dummy?" she asked Buddy.

So out of the store they walked: Gertie with her new red coat and hat, the chimps and Dick with all the red neckties, and Buddy, of course, wearing the biggest, brightest necktie in the store. By now newspaper photographers were following them, taking pictures of everything they did.

They went on a buggy ride through Central Park and had tea at the Plaza Hotel. Then they went to the movies at Radio City Music Hall, the biggest movie theater in the world.

Buddy and the chimps sat quietly through the cartoons and the newsreel. But when the Tarzan movie came on they went wild. Finally, as Tarzan battled an alligator in the jungle river, Buddy stood up and let out a jungle roar that nearly had the theater in a panic.

"I'm very sorry," said Gertie to the theater manager as he asked them to leave. "He's very sensitive about water. I should have thought of that."

The theater manager agreed but gave them each a lollipop as they left. Buddy's was especially large, and it was of course red.

By the time Dick had driven them home they were exhausted. The chimps had all fallen asleep. Buddy was snoring loudly in the back seat, his lollipop still clutched tightly in his giant hand. There were red neckties everywhere.

Bill walked up to the car and looked in the window.

"We had a red-letter day," Gertie whispered to him.

"Looks more like a red-necktie day," he said, smiling.

"You know where a four-hundred-pound gorilla sleeps?" asked Gertie.

"Anywhere he wants?" answered Bill.

"I'll get the tent and the sleeping bags," said Dick.

That night they camped out on the lawn, under a striped canopy tent they'd set up next to the car. There were overstuffed pillows everywhere and thick comforters covered in velvet. Lancelot slept on Beulah's lap and barked in his sleep, and Charlie sat perched on Dick's head. Bill snored contentedly between Lawrence, the dragon, and Boo, the leopard. The chimps and Buddy stayed in the car, asleep and unaware. Only Gertie was awake. She listened quietly to her father's old opera records on the Victrola.

Buddy stirred and looked out at her. He got out of the car and lumbered over sleepily. Gertie wrapped him in his red blanket. He fell back to sleep, his head in her lap.

Gertie felt as free and happy as she had when she was a girl in the forest, surrounded by her animals.

But deep inside she was still a little worried. Buddy was so big now. What if one day something upset him so much that even his red blanket or a red tie or a lollipop wouldn't calm him down?

Madcap Monkeys Make Manhattan Movie Matinee,"
read one headline in the newspaper the next morning.

"Simian Shoppers Show Snappy Fashion Sense" and
"Gorilla Gadabout Gallivants with Gal Named Gertie" were on
the front pages of the papers, along with pictures of Buddy and
Gertie.

The phone had not stopped ringing. People from all over the world had seen the stories and were anxious to see more of Gertie, Buddy, and the chimps.

"What's next, Hollywood?" asked Bill as they ate breakfast.

"No," replied Gertie, passing the bananas and earthworms to Buddy. "We've had an even better offer."

Nobody paid much attention. The chimps ate their cereal mixed with Jell-O. Beulah served up scrambled eggs and coconuts to Lawrence. The leopard lapped at his spaghetti and ice cream.

"We've been asked to have an exhibit at the World's Fair in Chicago!" Gertie announced. Everyone grew quiet.

The World's Fair was the place where nations from across the globe showed what was best about the past, the present, and the future. Millions of people would come. Newspapers, magazines, radio, and the newsreels would all tell stories about the amazing wonders on display. For that summer of 1933, the hopes, wishes, and dreams of the whole world would be focused on the fair.

Gertie looked at Bill imploringly.

"Well, we've got to go!" said Bill excitedly.

"We're gonna be famous now!" said Beulah.

"Ditto!" said Dick.

"Do you think Buddy will like it? Do you think he'll be O.K.?" asked Gertie.

"Gertie, ol' girl," Bill said to her. "Buddy loved New York, and New York loved him. I imagine the same will go for Chicago, and the world!"

"Chicago! Chicago! Chicago!" Charlie chirped and flew over to Gertie's shoulder.

"All right!" laughed Gertie. "Chicago it is."

So it was decided. They would go to the World's Fair.

The months leading up to the fair were a blur. Gertie had a million things to do. She told Bill what color to paint the Ape Pavilion, the place where they would live and perform at the fair. She told Beulah just how much food they might need. She worked out the chimps' routines with Dick and planned every little detail of their journey: what clothes to pack for the chimps, the special train car that would take them to Chicago—and how many extra red blankets they might need for Buddy.

"You've got to use cages," Bill told Gertie. "We can't risk them getting loose at the fair."

Gertie begrudgingly agreed. She'd sworn never to cage her animals, but if one of the chimps or Boo or, worst of all,

Buddy got loose, there was no telling what terrible things might happen.

So Gertie designed a beautiful cage for each chimp. Captain Jiggs's had a sailing motif. Maggie Klein's was covered with butterflies. Joe Mendi's was like an elegant Manhattan apartment.

But Buddy's was the grandest of all. His was like the tent of an Arabian sultan, filled with carpets and rugs and covered with drapes. You'd never have guessed it had bars.

Buddy loved his tent. Almost everything in it was red. He rolled happily on the thick oriental carpets and, on their first night at the fair, started a pillow fight with Gertie and the chimps.

"He's like the Sheik of Araby in that thing," said Bill. "He likes it so much we might have trouble getting him out of there."

"No," said Gertie. "Watch."

She stood outside the heavy iron gate and held up his red blanket.

"Here, Buddy," she called.

He looked up and rushed toward her so suddenly it almost frightened her. Gertie wrapped the blanket around

Buddy's head like a turban.

They all laughed.

"Now he *does* look like the Sheik of Araby," Dick laughed.

"He's Buddy, the Eighth Wonder of the World!" joked Bill.

"He's the silliest looking thing I ever saw," said Beulah.

The chimps beckoned Buddy back to the pillow fight. Bill, Dick, and even Beulah joined them. They played riotously. Gertie looked deep into Buddy's eyes. He seemed so happy.

"You're none of those things," she told Buddy. She kissed him lightly on the cheek and scratched him under his chin. "You're just my Buddy."

The fair was a happy mix of the miraculous and the silly. There was the "Hall of Tomorrow," a big, white, modern building filled with rocket ships and machines that would make the world of the future easy and carefree. There were robots who could do housework, beds that could make themselves, and even a gadget called the Brain-a-lator that was supposed to make you smarter. Next to the "Hall of Tomorrow" was an old-fashioned circus sideshow with exotic dancers, vaudeville comedians, magicians, and human oddities. There was even an antique roller coaster and a Ferris wheel.

Across from these was the "Avenue of Electricity," which showed the miracles of electric power, including Captain Electro and the world's largest light bulb. Then there were the "Streets of Many Lands," where each street looked exactly like a little strip of Paris, Rome, Dublin, or faraway Bombay. And right in the middle of the clutter of circus clowns and robots was the "Ape Pavilion."

Gertie, Buddy, and the chimps were a very popular attraction—even more popular than the world's largest light bulb. They had their own stage where they would perform and a glassed-in viewing hall where people could watch them in their special cages.

At first everybody had a wonderful time. Especially the chimps. They loved to perform and were happy with the attention and applause. Maggie Klein did a ballet dance and walked on a tightrope with Skippy. Joe and Captain Jiggs played drums and the banjo and sometimes tap-danced while Buddy would sit in a big easy chair and pretend to read the paper.

Thousands of people came to see them and millions more

read about them in newspapers and magazines. They were famous. Even Franklin Roosevelt, the President of the United States, came to visit.

But after a while Buddy seemed to grow bored with all the hubbub.

"He's unhappy," Gertie told Bill. "For the first time since we've had him, he's unhappy. I think he's been cooped up in his cage for too long."

The next day when Gertie opened Buddy's cage to check on him, Buddy jumped up suddenly and rushed for the door.

"Buddy, stop!" Gertie yelled, but he brushed right past her. Again she yelled for him to stop, but he didn't listen. He knocked open the door of the pavilion and ran out into the crowded streets of the fair.

Gertie shouted for Bill and the others.

Buddy wasn't hard to follow. Gertie could hear the screams of "Gorilla loose!"

She got a glimpse of Buddy as he headed toward the circus midway, but a frantic older gentleman grabbed her. "It's King Kong, lady!" he bellowed. "Run! Run!"

Buddy galloped from place to place at the fair. He paid no attention to the startled, screaming people. Happy to be free, he began to tear away his beautiful clothes. There was something in the air that drew him on, something that smelled familiar.

As he rounded the "Wonders of Bread" pavilion, he saw what he'd been searching for: a cluster of trees and undergrowth surrounding the "African Safari" ride.

He dove into the deep leafy palms and vines. He swung from limb to limb and rolled on the fern-covered ground. Then he sat very still in the dense junglelike shade. He sat there for a long, long time. He felt peaceful, happy, and strangely at home. Memories from long ago came back to him—his parents, his jungle home, and his childhood days.

Suddenly from all around him he could sense people closing in. He began to tremble. A single man was coming closer, then another and another. They were all holding guns. Buddy rose up to attack.

Then a familiar voice rang out.

"Get back, you nincompoops!" commanded Gertie. "And put away those stupid guns!"

Gertie was shoving her way through the heavy brush, past a line of policemen. She was clutching Buddy's red blanket.

"Get back!" she ordered, but the policemen only looked at her as if she were crazy. "He's *my* gorilla, and he's as gentle as a lamb," she told them.

Buddy watched her as she came closer. He stood stock-still, his eyes darting from Gertie to the policemen. Gertie held up the red blanket.

"Here, Buddy," she said firmly. "Come to Gertie."

The policemen stood at the ready, their guns pointed at Buddy.

"Come here!" said Gertie fighting to stay calm. "Buddy, you've got to come here. Please!"

Buddy relaxed his threatening stance and moved toward her. He reached out for the blanket. Gertie pulled him close to her.

"Good boy, Buddy," she gasped. "Good boy."

The policemen lowered their guns.

But it took hours to lure Buddy away from the African Safari ride. Only after Bill, Dick, and Beulah had found them were they able to coax Buddy back to the Ape Pavilion. They huddled around him while Gertie led the way.

He went willingly back into his cage, but as soon as Gertie closed the door, Buddy slammed his fists against the bars.

"What'll we do now, old girl?" asked Bill.

"I don't know," she said shaking her head. But in her heart she knew they would have to go home.

CHAPTER 7

They left the fair the very next day.

"I just hope we can control him back home," Gertie worried aloud.

"I just hope we can control him on the train," said Bill.

Buddy was fine on the train. They had their own baggage car. Buddy and the chimps ran around having pillow fights and enjoying themselves.

But back at their house in New York, Buddy was restless. He wouldn't stay in his room or go near his cage. He finally went to sleep in a huge oak tree in the backyard. Gertie camped out underneath the tree to make sure he didn't run away. She tried and tried to get him to come down. She held out his red blanket, but he snatched it away and kept it with him in the tree. She played her father's opera records for him. He listened intently but still wouldn't come down.

"It's not like it was when he was little," Gertie told Bill. "Back then I couldn't make him let go. Now I can't get him to come near me."

It was a long, sad night. Gertie barely slept.

The next morning she let Buddy scrub the kitchen floor. It was one of his favorite jobs and was the only time he wasn't afraid of water. He'd get his bucket full of soapy water and scrub for hours, lost in thought. It always seemed to calm him. But he was so strong he could actually wear away the linoleum, so about once a month Gertie would have the kitchen floor replaced.

Now there was a brand-new floor for Buddy to scrub, and he went at it with a vengeance.

"He's gonna wear it out lickety-split," Beulah told Gertie later that day.

Gertie decided to check on Buddy, but when she walked into the kitchen, she slipped on the wet floor. Her legs slid out in front of her, accidentally knocking over Buddy's bucket, and she landed with a loud thud. Water from the bucket splashed onto Buddy's face and soaked his head.

Gertie felt a little silly sitting on the floor, but she wasn't hurt. She managed to laugh at herself. Then she looked at Buddy. His face dripped with water. For a moment she thought he was making a funny face. Then she realized something was wrong—very wrong. Buddy looked angry.

Gertie remembered how Buddy had been afraid of water when he was little, but now *she* was afraid.

"Buddy, are you O.K.?" she asked gently.

He stood completely still for what seemed like a long time.

Then he rose up to his full height and let out a great furious jungle scream. Gertie's blood ran cold. She knew she was in trouble. She wasn't sure why, but somehow the water had done something to Buddy. This wasn't the sweet gorilla that she had raised. In one terrible moment, Buddy had turned wild.

Gertie crawled carefully out of the kitchen. Just as she quickly shut and locked the door, Buddy charged. He smashed against the door and splintered it open.

"Knock knock, who's there," chirped Charlie from his cage.

Gertie was shocked. She backed away slowly as Buddy came closer to her. She reached for his red blanket, which was draped over a chair. She held it out. Her hand was shaking.

Buddy ignored the blanket and threw the broken door across the room with one hand, almost hitting her.

Gertie was sure that he would charge again, but instead he knocked over a chair, then hurled a table with all his might against the wall. He began to break everything in the room—desks, lamps, statues, pictures on the wall, even a huge globe.

By then the whole house heard the commotion and stood watching, horrified, from the door.

Buddy looked over and rushed like a demon toward them.

"No, Buddy! No!" Charlie squawked. "No, Buddy! No, Buddy!"

Buddy stopped. Charlie chirped on. Buddy turned and

stared at Charlie. He seemed confused. He looked around the room as if amazed by what had happened.

Gertie walked cautiously toward him.

"It's O.K., Buddy," she said calmly.

He sat down on the floor and rocked back and forth. Gertie wrapped the blanket around his shoulders and hugged him.

"It'll be O.K., Buddy," she said softly.

Bill, Beulah, Dick, and the others walked cautiously toward them.

"What on earth happened?" Bill asked, his voice almost a whisper.

"I've never seen him like that," murmured Dick.

"He went wild on us," said Beulah.

"Poor Buddy," squawked Charlie. "Poor Buddy."

Gertie tried to look into his eyes, but he would not look up.

"Poor Buddy," said Gertie almost crying. "He *did* go wild."

for days there was an unhappy quiet about the house. Workmen came to repair the room that Buddy had destroyed.

Gertie stayed lost in thought and hardly spoke to anyone. She'd visit Buddy in his cage, where she'd had to put him since the attack, but he sat in a corner wrapped in his blanket with his back to anyone who came to see him. Gertie pleaded with Buddy to come to her, but he ignored her orders.

Gertie didn't know what to do. Buddy was miserable, but she couldn't let him run loose anymore.

"I promised I'd never cage my animals," she said to Buddy sadly. "I'll find a way, Buddy. I promise."

So she worried and thought and puzzled for days. Bill and Dick and Beulah and all the animals did their best to be cheerful. They dressed up and performed a dance to Gertie's opera records. But Buddy yanked down the curtains from his cage and turned his back to them. He slouched against the bars, his head hung low. It was as if he didn't like his home anymore.

Later, as Gertie leafed through her photo album, she found a picture of Buddy the day she'd picked him up at the zoo. He had been so tiny, sick, and frail, nestled in his box as the zookeeper carried him out to the car. Something in the picture got Gertie thinking. Behind the zookeeper there was a big, overgrown area of palm and banana trees.

She stared at the picture. And she remembered how hard it was to make Buddy leave that small plot of fake jungle at the World's Fair. A smile spread across her face. Her spirits lifted. She had an idea.

Six weeks later, a small caravan of covered trucks left the Lintz house headed toward Philadelphia. In the front truck rode Beulah and a host of household animals: Boo, the leopard; Lawrence, the dragon; and Lancelot. The little dachshund was wearing sunglasses for the drive. Charlie, the parrot, kept calling, "Take a left! Take a left!"

Dick drove the second truck with the chimps. Maggie sat in the front and blew kisses to passing cars while Joe Mendi, Captain Jiggs, and Skippy played in the back. In the third and last truck rode Gertie and Buddy. They sat quietly together while Bill drove.

Buddy clutched his red blanket. He craned his huge neck and peered out under the canvas truck cover. The world was rushing by as they sped along. Buddy sniffed the air and began to rock back and forth.

"It'll be O.K.," Gertie whispered to Buddy. "It'll be O.K., I promise."

After a while the trucks came to a stop. Then Gertie looked out from beneath the canvas cover. The zookeeper was greeting them at the gate of the zoo.

"Everything's ready," he told Gertie. "Just follow me."

They followed the zookeeper's car past cage after cage of animals. Buddy peered out again. He did not like what he saw.

Then they turned into a big open area that looked like a sort of park. You could barely see the high stone wall that surrounded it. They came to a stop.

The zookeeper called out, "We're here!" Gertie and Buddy could hear the sounds of the others getting out of their trucks. The chimps were laughing. Beulah was grousing, "Come on, leopard! Come on, lizard! Come on, everybody!" Charlie was chirping, "Nice spread! Nice spread!"

Gertie smiled at Buddy and gently took his hand.

"Come on," she said quietly. "Let's see your new home."

She led him out of the truck and into the sunlight. Everyone stood waiting and watching. Buddy looked slowly around. In every direction there were tall trees, and around them, bushes, palms, and ferns. It was beautiful, green, lush, and shady. It was almost like a jungle.

Buddy rocked back and forth excitedly and sniffed the air.

"Let's give him a chance to get used to it," Gertie said.

Suddenly in the distance two other gorillas came cautiously out of the woods.

"Here are your new friends, Buddy. We had them brought in just for you," Gertie told him.

Buddy stared at the gorillas. He hadn't seen others of his kind since he was a baby. He looked at Gertie.

"They're your new friends, Buddy," she said. Tears filled her eyes. "Go on. Go say hello!"

Buddy ran a circle around his old family, looking at Beulah and Dick and Bill and the chimps. He beat his chest joyfully.

Then he ran full speed toward the other apes but, just as suddenly, he halted.

He ran back to Gertie one last time.

She scratched under his chin and hugged him.

"Go on, you silly old thing," she said quietly. "I told you I'd make everything O.K."

She looked into his great dark eyes. "You're still such a mystery," she said and kissed him on the cheek. He took his red blanket from her hand and galloped toward the other apes.

Buddy disappeared into the verdant shade of the trees with his new gorilla pals.

"The zookeeper says we can come anytime we want," Gertie told the others.

"Good, maybe they've got a cage for Dicky Boy," joked Beulah.

"I'm house-trained and everything," said Dick.

The chimps rolled around and around in the grass.

"Maybe we could just move in here," quipped Bill. "It's not that different from our house."

"You're right, Bill. It's not that different," Gertie said. They all chuckled, then grew quiet as they watched Buddy swing happily through the trees with his new friends.

And so a long time ago in the 1930's, you might have seen many amazing things, for it was an amazing time. And if you'd gone to a zoo in Philadelphia on just about any weekend, you might have seen one of the most amazing things of all: a beautiful woman and her family having a picnic inside the gorilla domain. The woman's name? Gertie Lintz, of course. And her family? Bill, Dick, Beulah, and the chimps. And sometimes Lawrence the dragon and Boo the leopard and even little Lancelot the dachshund. A green parrot named Charlie would likely be chirping along to the opera music on the Victrola.

And way off in the distance, back in the trees, you might just make out a big gorilla with a red blanket. That, of course, was Buddy, far away from Africa to be sure, but at last very much at home.

AFTERWORD

Mrs. Lintz was the most famous dog breeder of her day. But it is for
her apes that she is remembered. On her Brooklyn estate she raised
over a dozen chimpanzees and two gorillas, in addition to hundreds
of other animals. She brought up her apes as much like humans as
possible. They wore clothes, played croquet, ate at the dinner table,
and did in fact go to the World's Fair of 1933. Her chimps went on to
star in the Tarzan movies, and appeared in Our Gang and The Three
Stooges short films. One of her gorillas became the main attraction
of the Barnum & Bailey Circus for many years. The gorilla depicted
in this book resided at the Philadelphia Zoo until 1984. He lived to
the ripe old age of fifty-four.